Conscious Parenting Using A Course in Miracles

Written by
Teri L. Hooper

I would like to thank my children Kristin, Kevin, and Shawn. They are and continue to be great teachers. I would also like to thank my husband Paul for his patience and understanding.

I would also like to thank my daughter Kristin and my grandchildren Austin and Aubree for contributing to the cover of this book.

Table of Contents

Forward   9

Chapter One – A Course In Miracles   11

Chapter Two - Infancy Through 18 Months   17

1. Colicky Babies
2. Weird Sleep Schedules
3. Nursing Versus Bottles
4. Introducing Solids
5. Teething
6. Naps

Chapter Three - 18 Months Through Age 4   27

1. Toilet Training
2. Temper Tantrums
3. Destructiveness
4. Reality Versus Fantasy

Chapter Four - Age 4 Through Age 7   35

1. Peer To Peer Disagreements

2. Tattling
3. Parents' Need For Excellence
4. Lying

Chapter Five - Age 8 Through Age 11   43

1. Sneaky Behavior
2. Meanness
3. School Problems
4. Friends
5. Technology

Chapter Six - Age 12 Through Age 14   55

1. Raging Hormones
2. Independence
3. Friends
4. Technology
5. Attitude
6. Peer Pressure
7. More Sneaky Behavior

Chapter Seven - Age 15 Through Age 18   69

1. Reasonableness
2. More Independence

3. Encouragement Without Interfering
4. Sexuality
5. More Sneaky Behavior

Chapter Eight - Age 19 Through Age 25 77

1. Ego-centric AGAIN
2. Letting Go
3. Pooper Scooper
4. Tying Up Loose Ends
5. Mental Illness

Chapter Nine - Adult Children 85

1. Helping, But Not Too Much
2. Staying In Your Own Yard
3. Giving Up Judgments
4. Grandchildren
5. Mental Illness

Chapter Ten - And So It Is 91

Forward

As I sat down to write this book, I made a decision that I was not going to worry about whether I was grammatically correct. I wasn't going to worry about whether I sounded like a simpleton or a scholar. I wanted to write from my heart and that is what I did.

When I approached every problem in this book, I went into meditation first. I surrendered the issue to the Holy Spirit for healing and guidance. I spent as much time as I needed until I felt I had the correct answer for my book. That is what I wrote.

If you feel the suggestions for handling a particular problem is not right for you, don't use them. I am in no way suggesting that my thoughts on an issue are the only solution. There are many ways to handle things and if your guidance tells you something else, then listen.

All adults and children are different. What works for one child may not work for another. Be flexible. Keep trying things until you find one that feels right. Surrender your frustrations to the One Mind within. Relax!

Chapter One

A Course In Miracles

I would like to start by saying I did none of the things suggested in this book when I was raising my children. I did not know **A Course in Miracles** existed. **A Course in Miracles** came into my life when my children were adults. It would have been nice to have the exposure to the **Course** and its principles back then though. I would have made very different decisions I'm sure.

When raising my personal children I relied on my educational training. I have a Bachelor's Degree in Elementary Education with a minor in Human Development. My minor included several classes in Marriage and the Family. I also have a Master's Degree in Curriculum and Instruction. I tried to raise and nurture my children with principles that I thought would make them successful from an educational aspect. I now know that pushing my children to excel did not produce the results I thought. I tried too hard to control their lives and sheltered them from experiencing the consequences of their decisions. They did not develop their own inner guidance until much later in their lives because I took control of their thought systems, or so I thought.

I also did not understand that my husband would have different ideas on how to raise our children. Because the two of us had very different thoughts about what to do with issues that came up regarding our children, they received a mishmash of direction and boundaries. We both believed our own thoughts were right about what was best for our children. I remember my own parents disagreeing about what was best for me. I received different messages from each of them. As I look around at the students I once had in my classroom along with my own children, I believe most people are raised with a mishmash of ideas. And perhaps that is ok.

This book is about using the principles of **A Course in Miracles** as a guidepost for interacting with children, mostly in a parental role. The ideas in this book came to me during meditation and times of quietness. Meditation allows the creative forces within to manifest into thoughts. It's those thoughts that I am drawing on that produced this book.

No matter what the situation is you are dealing with in regards to your children, the first thing on your "to do" list is to turn inwards and get in contact with the Holy Spirit within you. Then surrender your thoughts about the issue to the Holy Spirit admitting that you do not know what anything means. Be still for about one to two minutes without thinking if possible. Often the solution will be presented to you. If however it is not, I am offering some suggestions based on insights or guidance I received from the Oneness of all.

Raising children is not easy. Parenting does not come with a manual to help with specific situations that will arise from infancy to adulthood. Parents resort to using the same techniques that their parents used, even if those are things they do not like or approve of.

Parents usually shoot from the hip. They seldom pre-plan what they will do in certain situations. Reactionary parenting often results in remorse where parents wish they had done something different than what they actually did. It may teach parents lessons so they react differently the next time a similar situation occurs but often the parental mistake happens over and over until a new way of reacting to the problem occurs.

Generation after generation often repeats the failures of the past because they don't know any better. Their hearts are full of love and they want to do what is best but they lack the knowledge to enact that change. I believe that if the adults of this world had the knowledge that **A Course in Miracles** teaches, things would be different.

A Course in Miracles is a complete self-study spiritual thought system. As a three-volume curriculum consisting of a Text, Workbook for Students, and Manual for Teachers, it teaches that the way to universal love and peace—or remembering God—is by undoing guilt through forgiving others. The **Course** thus focuses on the healing of relationships and making them holy. **A Course in Miracles** emphasizes that it is but one version of the universal curriculum, of which there are "many thousands." Consequently, even though the language of the **Course** is that of traditional Christianity, it expresses a non-sectarian, non-denominational spirituality. **A Course in Miracles** therefore is a universal spiritual teaching, not a religion.

A Course in Miracles was "scribed" by Dr. Helen Schucman through a process of inner dictation she identified as coming from Jesus. A clinical and research psychologist and tenured Associate Professor of Medical Psychology, she was assisted by Dr. William Thetford, her department head, who was also a tenured Professor of Medical Psychology at the Medical Center where they both worked.

This *Course* can therefore be summed up very simply in this way:

> "Nothing real can be threatened.
> Nothing unreal exists.
> Herein lies the peace of God."

Chapter Two

Infancy Through 18 Months

At this stage of development children are totally dependent on the adults in their lives. They are unable to make decisions or think in terms of themselves and their world. Infant children live in the present moment. That is something they can teach the adults in their lives. They simply react to whatever they are feeling right now. Their behaviors are directed by instinct.

Babies require a lot of attention and a lot of action by parents or guardians. This can be emotionally and physically draining on the caregivers. Turning to **A Course in Miracles** as a way to stay grounded during this time in a baby's and an adult's life. It can make this period a bit smoother and less exhausting.

A Course in Miracles says that this world is only our perception. According to the **Course** our minds created everything we perceive. That means we created the idea of a baby and us being parents. That's a big blow to our ego self that wants this experience to be more than that.

1) Colicky Babies

When you as a parent are up with a colicky baby at two o'clock in the morning, trying to convince yourself that this is an illusion and isn't real will make you want to throw the **Course** book across the room in disgust. That's totally understandable.

Step One with any situation involving children of any age is to take a couple breaths and surrender the situation to the Holy Spirit within you. You are always connected to God because you are part of God. Therefore you have within you the means to create a solution to ANY problem you may be facing.

Colicky babies are reacting to the sensations around them. In the womb they are protected and guarded from outside stimulation. However, after birth, the entire world is exposed to their little bodies. Their intestines are just learning to break down and utilize the milk they are consuming. They are having feelings inside their bodies of pain and pleasure that they are not familiar with. So when they cry out, it can be because of many different things.

When thinking about what to do with a colicky baby while believing in **A Course in Miracles**, one has to start by changing how we think about the situation. A miracle is defined as a shift in perception. The first and most important step is that we have to change how we view things.

The crying colicky baby is part of the One Child of God. In form it does not seem so but in Truth it is. Looking at that beautiful baby and seeing that he or she is perfect and whole, regardless of what he or she is doing at the moment can help you relax and then do what you can to solve the problem. That child and you are One and therefore if you give LOVE to yourself, you are giving LOVE to the child.

Colicky babies are often over-stimulated. To feel secure and safe, they crave the feeling of the womb. In the maternity wards of hospitals, the nurses know that to simulate the feeling of the womb, newborns need to be swaddled. A colicky baby will often settle down if parents will practice the 5 S' System by Dr. Harvey Karp. His book can be found online or in most bookstores.

2) Weird Sleep Schedules

Another common problem with babies is getting them to sleep through the night. Once again if we choose to look at the situation differently, take a few breaths, try to see the baby as a perfect Child of God (and not the awake baby at two o'clock in the morning) we diffuse many of our emotions caused by fatigue.

Newborns' needs are different than those of older babies. They need to eat every couple hours between the ages of birth to three months. Wanting them to sleep through the night at this stage of their development is not realistic. Their little stomachs cannot hold that much which is why they need to eat frequently. As they get older, they will be able to eat larger amounts of breast milk or formula enabling them to sleep for longer and longer periods. Don't try to rush things. According to the **Course**, things will happen in exactly the right time so try not to let your fatigue control your mind. You alone control your mind!

During this stage of development, children go through tremendous growth. When they start to teethe, schedules get thrown off and a sweet happy baby often becomes a cranky, irritable baby. Again, follow the basics of the **Course**. The behavior you see on the outside is not what God knows about your child. Your child is preciously perfect exactly as he or she is. Relax, take a few breaths, and surrender to the Holy Spirit within you asking for the best way to handle things. You usually won't receive "words" telling you what to do. You will get a "gut" feeling that is loving and that is the place from which you will do what you feel is right to do.

3)   Nursing Versus Bottle Feeding

This debate has been going on for years. Truthfully, there is no right or wrong answer. Every parent has to look within for guidance when they are deciding the kind of feeding that feels best for their child. If their choice feels right then it is right!

In most cultures, parental and peer opinions cause a great amount of consternation. Parents often feel inadequate because they are not doing what society is telling them to do. The **Course** would suggest that you are creating the world you perceive. That means you are creating the opinions of others. Do not attach to those opinions. Release them to the Holy Spirit admitting that you do not know what anything means. Those opinions will be healed instantaneously even if in the world of form it looks like nothing has happened. What matters is that you feel better and releasing those negative feelings to Spirit allows you to feel better about your decision.

4)   Introducing Solids

When babies are introduced to solids has changed over many generations. Solids used to be a way to help babies sleep for longer periods of time. Whether that was a benefit for the baby or the parent is in question. Regardless, introducing solids too soon is frowned upon these days.

Science and research now tells us that babies' digestive systems can't handle solids much before six months. However, that is a difficult thing for parents to adhere to. Many parents start solids before six months without problems. Again, turn within and ask for guidance. Ask yourself, do you want to add solids to your child's diet because you feel he/she is ready for that or do you want to add solids to help with sleeping through the night? The truth is when your baby is thirty-five years old, whether they started solids at four, five, or six months won't have mattered.

5)   Teething

Teething is not necessarily hard but parents struggle to watch their babies suffer with teething pain. Babies do not understand pain so to cope with it, they become irritable.

They do not have the verbal skills to communicate to adults the pain they are feeling so all they can do is cry.

For parents knowing what to do to soothe a baby in pain is unsettling. Loving your child through the pain of teething can be difficult. Be easy on yourself. Give yourself a minute or two to think about what you feel needs to be done. Guidance will come if you are open to receive it.

Love your child and provide ways to dull the pain. Baby pain medication can be obtained over the counter at any drug or grocery store. Frozen teething rings can provide a numbing effect. Topical medications can be applied directly to the gums for relief. Be careful to read the directions to make sure you are using the correct amount of medication for your child's age.

When your baby is sleeping, try to do something nice for yourself. Too often new parents use a baby's naptime to catch up on housecleaning or other chores. That is fine to do some of the time but don't forget to allow times of rest for rejuvenating your parental juices. It's like what you are instructed to do on an airplane in case of a loss of cabin pressure. But the mask on yourself FIRST, then put it on your child. You have to take care of yourself to be able to take care of your baby.

6)   Naps

This is an area I see parents stress over needlessly. They try to control their baby's nap times trying to make them work around the parents' schedules. This is like trying to swim out to sea against the waves. In the end, the naptime is never controlled and the parent is never happy.

As adults we know there are times when we go to bed and lay there unable to fall asleep. While frustrating, we know that is common. However, when our baby won't take a nap when we think he/she should, we are upset. This is a double standard. Perhaps your baby is not ready for sleep. Let your child remain awake until you are given cues such as crankiness to signal when naptime is appropriate. If that means your child will nap in the car or at the grocery store, so be it. As the adult in the situation, you should be the one working around your child's sleep schedule. Don't go to the department store to try on clothes when you know your child will be ready for a nap in the near future. You are asking for an unpleasant experience.

Relax. Try to ask Holy Spirit for guidance when you feel a struggle of any kind. The **Course** says you walk with God in perfect holiness. If what you are doing comes from LOVE then there can be no error. Later in life when you are playing BINGO in a senior citizen center the struggle with naptimes will be but a blur.

During the infant stage, keeping your child safe from harm, fed, cleansed, along with giving love, is what you primarily will do. If you feel something may be wrong like your child is sick, you seek medical attention. Remember that your child is part of the Sonship that you are also a part of. Your child is not your possession. He or she is tethered to the Christ consciousness that we all are. As long as you see your child as part of God and you ask that all your errors in perception regarding that baby in your arms be healed, they will be. Relax and enjoy the ride!

Chapter Three

18 Months Through Age 4

Raising children at any age is a bumpy ride. Every stage of development has its good and bad. The good news is that we get to choose how we want to see things at any given moment. The knowledge of that freedom will get you through any stage of this form we all live.

This period of a child's life is often referred to as the toddler stage. During this time, your child is walking, learning language, talking, and experiencing the world around them. Their intellectual development is growing in leaps and bounds. But, it has many limitations.

Toddlers are unable to think in terms of another person's position. They cannot put themselves into another person's shoes. That means that even though they can be trained to "share" they do not understand the need to share. Toddlers cannot see the world from any position except their own. Asking a two year old to share a toy and to understand the need to share a toy is unrealistic. When two toddlers want to play with the same toy, asking them to share will seldom work. Understanding their limitations cognitively can avoid many unpleasant experiences. In a situation where two toddlers want the same toy the best advice I can recommend is to try to divert their attention to another toy and when the time is right, remove the toy in conflict from the scene altogether. Luckily, toddlers have short attention spans and the toy can be slyly put back into the play area later.

A Course in Miracles suggests that these children are part of the One Mind so we adults should always attempt to see the Christ Consciousness in them, not the seemingly silly behavior of two individual toddlers fighting over the same toy. Remembering that they are the Light of the World, as are we, will help us know that however we choose to fix a worldly problem, things will always be alright.

1) Toilet Training

When a child is officially "toilet trained" has become a status symbol in mom circles. Parents often brag about the best way to do it or at what age it should happen. Let me assure you that I have never come across a child who was NOT toilet trained when they entered kindergarten! This topic is one that causes way too much stress on parents.

The general rule is that the longer you wait to attempt toilet training, the quicker it happens. Many children are not ready until they are close to three years old. I know that horrifies many parents because they are concerned with the perception of others. Don't be! The **Course** states "in my defenselessness my safety lies." What that suggests is that you should not defend against anything that is going on in your life. The more you stress out about whether or not your child is toilet trained at the same time as your friend's child who is of a similar age, the more stress you create for yourself. As "Frozen" Elsa sings, "Let It Go!"

The **Course** would remind us that things happen in Divine right time. Keeping this in your mind reminds you to gently introduce the potty but not push. Your child will resist if you push. Just allow it to be with easy encouragement.

2) Temper Tantrums

Who doesn't know about the "terrible twos?" Many parents will tell you it can also be the "terrible threes." Whenever it is, it is challenging for parents. Tantrums come for many reasons and those can be avoided with some reasonable planning. For example, don't take a child this age out after lunch. They are tired after lunch and usually need a nap. I can't tell you how many times I see moms and their toddlers out at Target or the grocery store and their child is crying hysterically. It's usually because they are tired. Tired toddlers are not happy toddlers. If you want to cut back on the number of tantrums, stay home during the early afternoon.

There are however many more tantrums where a cause is not apparent. Remembering that your child is not your possession is helpful during stressful tantrum times. The **Course** often refers to us as being insane. It says we are all insane and that means that our toddlers are insane but in a different way than us. Our insane behavior takes on characteristics of adults whereas our toddler's behavior takes on its own characteristics. It's okay. We don't have to understand.

The best way to deal with a tantrum is to initially see if there is something that will soothe your child. Perhaps your child needs to be held. Perhaps your child needs to have a snack. However, if after a few loving attempts to minimize the tantrum has failed, the only way forward is to allow the tantrum to happen as it needs to. Your role during the tantrum is to help prevent injury to your child if needed. Other than that, just sit back and watch the show!

Many times the tantrum is more about them needing attention. The conundrum that arises is that if you give too much attention during a tantrum, that sends the message to your child that having a tantrum is the way to get attention. The **Course** reminds us that the Son of God had a tiny mad idea that he could be separate from his Father. We forgot to laugh at that tiny mad idea. During a toddler temper tantrum remind yourself to laugh!

3)   Destructiveness

Toddlers can be human tornadoes. They have such short attention spans that they flit from toy to toy, activity to activity creating a line of destruction and messes along the way. They do not understand the idea that things break. Trying to manipulate whatever is in their possession results in it breaking. I have watched parents keep precious trinkets out on the coffee and end tables only to have their toddler destroy it. If you do not want your valuables broken to pieces, put them away. There will come a time when you can bring them out for public viewing again without the fear of them being destroyed.

Looking at valuables from a **Course** perspective, they have no meaning in Truth anyway. They have meaning in the ego's perspective only. Loving your possessions without attachment is the goal here. If protecting them from your Tasmanian Devil is needed, do it. Putting them up and away from your toddler will make life much more pleasant for you and your child.

Many parents feel a need to clean up after the destructiveness that is happening continuously. Unless your goal is to be in a perpetual state of exhaustion, I would not recommend this. First off, they can pull everything out of the toy box faster than you can put it away. My suggestion is to wait until naptime and bedtime to pick up the toys that are out. If at those times you are tired, leave them be. There will come a time when this is not a concern. Have faith in that and try to enjoy the chaos of the present moment.

4)   Reality Versus Fantasy

The toddler phase is a time of experimentation. It's also a time where the line between reality and fantasy is blurred. Sometimes I think toddlers understand **A Course in Miracles** better than adults do. This blurriness creates situations where anything is possible and reality is in the eye of the beholder. Toddlers have such a vivid imagination that they often choose what they want to see or experience. That is **Course** 101 curriculum. Parents take notice!

Our job as adults is to allow their perception of their world to be exactly as it is. It would be preferable for parents to jump into this pool of make-believe with them. Since the *Course* says the world is our perception, who is to say their projection of the world isn't any worse or better than ours? Trying to force your reality onto a toddler is ego craziness. Surrender knowing that when your child is thirty-five it won't have mattered. According to the *Course*, we're all insane anyway!

Chapter Four

Age 4 Through Age 7

As an educator and a mother, this is one of my favorite times of childhood. This age is sweet, smart, aware, and yet naïve. Children of this age can have compassion for others. They are loving, genuinely helpful and very forgiving. The biggest mistakes parents make during this phase of development is to hold on too tight. Parents try too hard to control childhood situations thus forcing outcomes that are pleasing to the parent but not to the child.

1) Peer To Peer Disagreements

An example of this would be a disagreement between a couple children during play. Children at this age are more than capable of solving problems that arise with their peers that meet their satisfaction. However as parents observe the discourse going on, they often don't think the resolution agreed upon is fair from an adult's perspective. They try to interfere with the negotiations between the children and persuade them to agree to a solution that meets the adult's idea of fair. This ultimately teaches children that they are incapable of conflict resolution. Later on, that produces children who lack the confidence to take care business!

From **A Course in Miracles** teachings, all perspectives (both those of the adults and those of the children) are not correct because they are coming from the ego mind, are illusions and are not real. Therefore, imposing an adult opinion on children is no more correct than either of the child's opinions. What matters in this situation is how each party involved feels. If the children are happy with the agreed upon solution, they are operating from a place of peace and are therefore connected to God. The solution is not the goal. The feeling of peace, love and joy are. Even if one child is not happy about the outcome, it is usually forgotten once play has resumed. Adults, however, have more developed egos so they hold on to grievances longer than children. Yet, adults have the same ability to feel peace, love and joy if they so choose. The **Course** emphasizes that we can always choose again to feel the peace of God. Let the kids be happy and choose the same for you.

2) Tattling

Children this age have a very black and white sense of this world. They have an idealistic view of the adults they are exposed to. Teachers, parents, police, doctors, literally everyone in a big body never make mistakes in their view. Children at this stage of development also believe that justice will always be done which is why tattling is common at this age. They think that every perceived wrong action must be held to account for justice to be served. If a teacher or parent does not see an error in behavior, the child feels it is their moral duty to report it so that punishment can be assigned. For the adults this is maddening! For the child, this is necessary!

As a teacher, I found myself constantly listening to my first graders tattle on one another. Even though I wasn't a *Course* student while I was teaching, I treated these events in a way that is in line with *Course* thinking. When students would tattle I would ask them, "What are you going to do about that?" First off, that would totally throw them for a loop because typically adults take charge of the situation when a child tattles. My students would give me a variety of responses to my question. I was careful not to show an opinion or judge their ideas. They would soon decide upon a course of action on their own. A lot of children would go tell the other misbehaving child that they did not like what they were doing. Sometimes the disagreeable child would stop the disagreeable action. Other times they wouldn't. In the second case, the tattling child usually went to play somewhere else or went about their business and within a few minutes the issue was forgotten. It was as if it didn't occur which according to the *Course* it didn't!

3) Parents' Need For Excellence

Children at this age grow intellectually in leaps and bounds. One day they barely know their alphabet, the next day they are reading and writing paragraphs. Because they are growing so fast parents often get very excited and push too hard, too fast to excel. Even though parents who push their children mean well, it often has different results from those that are hoped for.

The *Course* states "In my defenselessness my safety lies." When parents are pushing their children to succeed, they are defending their perception of worthiness as a parent. They believe that they are helping their children be better than other children. The *Course* says we are One with our creator and no one is more special than another. When parents believe their child can be a better student than another child, they are defending the specialness of an individual.

This push to excel also starts to show up in extra-curricular activities, especially in sports. A child may show a casual interest in a sport and the next thing you know that child is signed up for the season and has the uniform! Parents also tend to push activities that they themselves like or were good at. I have often seen a child crying in the outfield while a parent is yelling at them because they don't want to play the game or be at the practice.

What I want to suggest is that parents look within to see if their motivations are for their child or themselves. If your child is interested in baseball, let them play a season. Part of teaching responsibility is letting your child know that if they sign up, they have to finish their commitment. Of course if something horrific is going on, pull your child from the activity immediately. However, as long as things are safe and straight forward, make sure your child finishes what they said they would do. After the season is over if they do not want to do baseball again, let it be over. As a parent you have to respect their decisions as long as they have followed through with their initial commitment.

The **Course** tells us that everything is a matter of perception. That includes your perception of the activity in relation to your child. Make sure you are in touch with how you're feeling. If you feel good about the decisions you are making in conjunction with your child around extra-curricular activities, then you together are making the Divine choice. If you feel a strain for whatever reason, then you are being led by your ego. Do what "feels" right!

Allowing our children to be exactly as they are and exactly as they are not is the aim as a *Course* parent. By turning inward and surrendering to the Holy Spirit, guidance will usually come and you will know what the right action to take is. If you feel bad at the thought of doing something, it is not the correct action. However, if the action makes you feel good or at peace, it is Divinely correct.

4) Lying

Lying happens before this age however it is not understood as an untruth when it occurs in toddlers. By the age of 5 the child is usually aware of whether what they are telling is a lie or not. Plainly put . . . they know they are lying!

This is very frustrating for parents and most parents will try to stop the lying. They often become more controlling or intrusive in an attempt to stop a lie. This is such a waste of energy and it produces very little for the amount of stress it causes. The *Course* tells us that we can barely control ourselves much less another person. The appropriate response to lying is to let it be. If you happen on the facts that a lie has occurred, it's okay to mention your knowledge of the facts to you child. Then, let it go.

Sometimes though, we allow our ego to defend against the action that we think feels appropriate. The right action can be viewed by our ego mind as the wimpy way out or not being aggressive or controlling enough. Remember to notice how you feel in your gut. If it feels uneasy regardless of what your mind is thinking then it is not the right choice. And the good news is, if it is the wrong choice, you can always choose again!

Chapter Five

Age 8 Through Age 11

This age of development is where your child is starting to show signs of who they really are. Their strengths and weaknesses are starting to become obvious. The personality traits are characterizing them as individuals and many of these are not pleasant to the parent. Parents erroneously believe that they can change their children's undesirable behaviors by tightening control. Even if this were to work, the results are usually temporary. Children grow into the uniqueness that they are and that will include the bad with the good.

Too often parents view their children as possessions. Your children do not belong to you. They are God's expression of the One Mind. You as parents have an obligation to love, shelter, feed, and protect from harm. Protecting from harm is what most parents take to an extreme. Harm can be interpreted as many things to parents. Protecting a child from jumping off the roof would be an example of protection. Making sure they know how to swim before allowing them to jump off the boat into the lake would be another. But the truth is we can't protect our children from everything. Parents generally would agree to this statement but their actions usually prove otherwise. Life in form is cruel and often times horrific and even though parents try to shelter their children from the harshness of this worldly experience, in truth that can't be done.

I understand how heartbreaking this realization is to most people. It is heartbreaking to the ego but not to the part of the mind that knows the Truth of who we all are. The *Course* would tell you that the horrible possibilities of harm to your child is a story made up by your ego to keep you separate from God and also separate from your child. Of course this is not true. The things that happen in this world whether they are good or bad, are not seen by God. God knows not of this world. God knows only of the goodness of his One Son and that is you and your child. It is your ego that believes in the special relationship your ego mind has developed about your child. (I will talk more about special relationships in the teen section.)

The *Course* would tell parents that this is the time when you should start practicing seeing the light that is the essence of your child and not the behavior on the outside of the veil. Children like adults are insane according to the *Course* and when we as parents begin to judge the antics of our children then we are showing our insanity.

1. Sneaky Behavior

During this phase of development, children realize that people get away with bad behavior and that justice doesn't always happen. This ignites the tiny mad idea that since others don't always get caught when they do something morally wrong, then perhaps they too can do things that their upbringing tells them they shouldn't and get away with it. This is when blatant lying begins and this is very frustrating for parents.

The good news is lying is usually a sign that the child has a moral compass. If they didn't they wouldn't lie because they wouldn't see anything wrong with whatever they are doing. The problem is not the lying. The problem is that parents tighten their grip or control to attempt to keep their children from lying or to try to teach that lying is morally wrong. Children this age know that lying is wrong but they do it anyway. Adults lie all the time too so expecting our children not to lie is hypocritical of us. According to the *Course*, lying is not the problem. What upsets us is that we believe the story that lying is occurring. We have made the story real and that is what causes us unease.

When we are feeling unease about what the ego perceives as a moral issue we have to ask ourselves if the story that is causing the discomfort is real. Of course, it never is if we are true *Course* students. So you might be asking what a parent should do. I can only tell you what guidance I have received in regards to this issue. By turning to your connection with God you might get a different message. Once again, go with what feels good when reacting.

From my experience with children, calmly telling them that you know a different truth than what they are telling you often stops the lie dead in its tracks. I don't recommend actually telling the child that you know they are lying but it's ok to let them know that you know a different story. Don't defend your knowing about the lie and don't force the child to defend their lie. At this age, children often continue to lie beyond the original lie to save face. By not directly calling them a liar, you are allowing the lie to simply be forgotten. Once caught in a lie, children want to find a way out. If you let them know what you know, they are smart enough to know they've been caught. Making them feel worse than they already do once they know you are aware of their lie serves no purpose. It does not keep them from lying again. In fact, they tend to lie more because a fear has been implanted in their minds and fear never produces anything positive. Children usually lie less when they feel a sense of understanding and love. They know it's safe to make a mistake.

2. Meanness

Meanness can begin to happen around this age. Children start to establish their own pecking order in their peer world. This is an ego behavior that is supported by society at large. I don't know if it's possible at this age to totally get rid of this ego thinking but I believe it's possible to provide another perspective to give your child pause for thought.

Now is the time in your child's life when your actions influence the thoughts of your child. Now is the time in your child's life when your thoughts about moral issues start to penetrate the mind of your child. You may not think they hear you but I guarantee that you are being heard. As much as is possible, make your thoughts known without judging or criticizing the behaviors of others. When your child starts to pass judgment on another, play devil's advocate. Point out another point of view your child may not have thought of. Do so with as much love and compassion for the criticized individual as is possible. And know with the soul of your being that the Truth of the judged and the judge is the same. Even though you alone will be thinking that all the parties in the discussion are part of the Sonship, your child will benefit from your knowledge of Truth because what you give you receive.

3. School Problems

This is the time when it is crucial that you allow your child to begin to experience the consequences of their actions. It is also a time when you should refrain from solving your child's problems when you can. When they refuse to do their homework let them experience whatever happens at school to those who do not do their homework. If they need help, do so only enough to get them started and then let them know you have confidence in their ability to do the rest on their own. Often children play manipulation games to try to get their parents to do more than they should. If your child seems not to understand what is expected of them calmly and lovingly suggest to your child that they explain to their teacher that they don't understand their work and ask for more instruction. If you can provide the needed instruction, do so. If the child is truly capable and just being lazy, they will complete their homework instead of admitting to their teacher that they lied to their parents about not understanding it in an effort to get out of doing it. If the child is being honest about their lack of understanding, you are teaching your child to admit that they need more instruction and that it is ok to do so without feeling inadequate.

Most of the time teachers are hard working, genuinely caring people who want the best for their students. However there can be exceptions but that need not be a negative ego experience. Even though as a parent you may not believe what you are saying, try to help your child see the good in the teacher regardless of what the teacher is doing. Your child will usually be much more forgiving of their teacher than you will be. As parents, we want to defend our children from adults in their world that may not have their best interests at heart whether it is teachers, coaches, or club leaders. If you remember from earlier in this book I mentioned that defending against anything only causes you pain and suffering. It also models for your child that they need to defend against another and experience pain and suffering as well. Do you really want that for your child?

I remember a minister from a church I attended once saying in a sermon, "You can never know everything that is going on in another person's life so you never have enough information to have an opinion or a judgment!" That has stuck with me for years. It's a message that would be good for parents to remember and instill in their children when it seems another is not acting in a way you think they should.

When a teacher does not react in a way that you as a parent think is the appropriate response remember that you do not know everything that is going on. Maybe your child is behaving in a way with that teacher that justifies the teacher's reaction. Maybe that teacher has something going on in their life that needs compassion and understanding. Maybe there's a political restriction that is creating a situation that makes the teacher believe that his/her behavior is the only option. Or maybe the teacher is just having a bad day. In most cases the situation that the parent believes is terrible is not the perspective of their child. Even if the child agrees with the opinion of their parent, often the child does not agree with the parent on the action that should be taken. Again, perspective is uniquely our own.

4) Friends

At this age friends are starting to become the most important people in your child's life. Your child is trying to figure out their place in this world and they are using friendships to help them. Most of the time this is nothing to be concerned about. They are learning what they can and can't do in relation to other children they are in contact with. If however, the friendship situation is not a healthy one, parents usually try to take control.

Hopefully, you are taking your parenting journey with much more emphasis on releasing problems to the Holy Spirit for guidance. You are open to receiving guidance on what is best to do. There are so many variables around friendship problems that an entire book could be written on this topic alone. Try not to be defensive and controlling. If you do, you will create additional problems from the ones you may be experiencing.

If the friendship your child is having is dangerous or destructive you may have to restrict interaction with the other child. If the other child is at the same school, trying to stop contact with the undesirable friend may not be possible.

Initially, the best tactic might be to calmly talk to your child about your concerns. This conversation has to be done very carefully because if your child suspects a hint of judgment it could backfire and make the undesirable child more desirable. Talk about behaviors you don't like and why you don't like them without mentioning the specific child who is doing them. Your child is old enough and smart enough to put two and two together but not judging your child's decision to be friends with this other child will take away the need for your child to have to defend his friendship decisions. The **Course** section about defenselessness applies to your child here. He/she may not know it but you are healing both your minds when you take away your child's need to defend him/her self.

5)   Technology

Today's advances in technology and its availability creates problems where there never used to be. Between computers, cell phones, and electronic tablets, trying to keep your child away from a screen can be a constant strain between parents and children. Trying to keep your child away from the technology of today is unrealistic. They are living in a world where knowing how to use technology is a must. And it is only going to become more widely used in the future.

So today's parents have to decide how much technology to allow. My guidance tells me to gradually phase it in. Having an emergency cell phone with parental limitations could be a beneficial thing. Cell phones at this age have NO place at school unless it remains turned off in a backpack only to be used in case of emergency.

The phone should have limits on when it can be used outside of school. Perhaps it can be used to socialize with friends after school and before seven o'clock at night. It has been my experience that when you allow something like this with parameters, the desire for it by your child lessens. Children at this age shouldn't be big spending a lot of time on the phone. They should be encouraged to use spare time playing and learning household chore and routines. If your child has enough things to occupy their free time, they won't want to spend time on a cell phone.

A computer or tablet is another story. Schools are using them more and more for instruction. In that situation, they can be good. However, there are so many games available and a vast amount of time can be wasted playing them. Often these games are used as babysitters so parents can accomplish the many things they need do. When they are being used to lessen the interaction between parents and children, they are detrimental. If however, they are used in moderation to help parents with their busy schedules, then they can be a bonus.

At this age, technology should be minimized through parental involvement with their child's activities. If you are unsure if the amount of time spent playing games is too much, turn within and ask. Holy Spirit will ease your burden by healing your mind. If you allow the Christ Consciousness within you to guide you, you will know exactly how much technology time is enough.

In any given situation, I'm not saying to do nothing if you believe the situation is extreme and needs action. I'm suggesting that you first ask for guidance from the Holy Spirit. Get quiet and perhaps take a long walk. Search within for what feels right to do and then do it with peace in your heart. When you act from this place instead of the place of emotions, you are Divinely guided along the correct course. And of course as stated before, if you choose wrongly, you can always choose again!

Chapter Six

Age 12 Through Age 14

What can I say about kids this age? It is challenging to say the least. One of my favorite sayings about this age group is that they are little kids in big bodies.

What's scary is that they are physically capable of my adult actions and behaviors. Why that's scary is because they don't know the consequences of many of those behaviors. Like with toddlers before they learn about the concept of fear, middle school-age children go around attempting things without being aware of the things they that could be detrimental to their physical well being.

1. Raging Hormones

This age is well into the "flirt-fest!" They have found the opposite sex or at least have started to feel their sexually blooming. They don't always know what to do with those raging urges and impulses but their hormones are sending many signals they have not experienced before.

From a *Course* perspective, we should give them to the hands of God to guide. However, in this world of form, we have to share that guidance with the Holy Spirit. The biggest challenge from a parent's point of view is to figure out how to help your child without taking over control.

Again, I will go back to what I have been saying continuously from the beginning. When confronted with a decision that needs to be made about an action that needs to be taken, get quiet and go within for guidance. Try to take as much time as is possible to surrender the situation to the Holy Spirit for healing and quietly allow inspiration to come in. Usually you will have a good idea of the best course of action to take. You can use the "feel" test. If it feels good it is probably Divinely inspired. If it doesn't then perhaps you should give it more time.

2. Independence

One of the issues that are difficult for most parents of this age is how much independence to allow. Kids in middle school want to exclusively hang around with their friends to the heartache of their parents. Children start desiring a life separate from the family that they have been so close to. Secrecy is a way they try to achieve that independence.

Parents start to know less and less about their friends and peer groups so it is not always known what kind of influences they are getting.

The important thing to note here is that as parents, you cannot control what influences they are exposed to anymore. To be honest, once they entered kindergarten you stopped being able to control that. Even if you homeschool them, they get influences from coaches, dance teachers, religious leaders, etc. According to the **Course**, they are not the special relationship that you believe they are. Here is probably a good time to discuss a little bit about the idea of special relationships.

The **Course** says that special relationships were created by the ego to keep us individuals and separate from God. In Truth, we are all part of the Oneness of God's Son, which includes your middle school-age kids. You only believe that your child is special to you but in Truth, they are not. They are not any more special than the homeless person on the side of the street. I know many of you are ready to close this book right now, but please don't!

Special relationships don't exist according to the **Course**, at least not in the way we think of them. Our children, our parents, our family, our friends, our co-workers, and any other groups of individuals that we believe we have a unique bond with are only an ego idea. Everyone is equal as a brother in the Sonship and no one has any more special status than another. As a grandmother and mother, I struggled with this idea more than any other in the **Course**. The Truth is my grandchildren are no more special to me than you who are reading this book. It was only my ego that was hurt by that idea. Once I understood that it was my ego that was holding on to the idea of my personal special relationships and I surrendered that erroneous thought to the Holy Spirit for healing, I could finally see everyone with the love equally.

In time letting go of the idea that anyone was more special than anyone else, I could just love my grandchildren and enjoy them. The test for me was learning to love everyone as much as I love my family. My focus shifted to learning to love everyone else with the same intensity as the love I felt for my special relationships.

The **Course** talks about viewing relationships as holy relationships. A holy relationship is a process, a gradual reversal of the special relationship. The reversal is changing the idea of your child being more special to you than anyone else to viewing your child with the exact same love you feel for anyone else.

Does this mean I know longer have to behave as if my family is in a different category as other people? Honestly yes, but realistically no. I will still spend more time with friends and family in the world of form. What will change is the way you look at them. Your perspective will be different.

Now that we understand that our children are not any more special in the Sonship than any other person, we can begin to look at them with a bit more independence. Just as we have to trust in God and the Holy Spirit within us, we have to begin to trust in our children when they are not with us. If along the way we have been demonstrating love in our actions and our words, we know our children will have this received this love. There's a good chance that the majority of the time our children will behave appropriately. From the **Course's** standpoint, it doesn't matter anyway. Behaviors in the world of form are of the ego and are immediately viewed as errors by the Holy Spirit and healed. In truth, the majority of mistakes you made at this age are of no significance later in life anyway.

That's not to say that you let your child run rough-shot all over town. You will find that you have to say no many times while you mentally remember the Oneness with your child.

Detach from the situation at the same time you are handling the situation. Seems crazy but it is possible.

3)   Friends

At this age no one matters except friends to your child. Friends become their idols and parents become the stupidest people in the world. Remember to not take anything they say or do personally. The **Course** often talks about the insanity of the world and the ego. Your new teenager is just a tad more insane than normal!

Talking to your newly teen is often delicate. They are seldom receptive to what you want to tell them. If you can find a way to talk to them from a neutral place without fault finding you will have more success. You would be surprised how much of what you say is actually heard by them, even if they won't admit it at the time.

Parenting a middle age school child requires good detective work and a little bit of sneakiness. You have to watch your child from afar. One way to get a feel for what kind of children their friends are is to be the house that everyone comes to. Let your child hang out with their friends at your house. Cook up some pizzas, buy a couple liters of soda and try to be a fly on the wall. Kids this age are naturally loud and obnoxious so you can eavesdrop on their conversations without much difficulty. Try not to judge the crazy things they say. Look at the big picture. Are the things they are saying and doing silly teen hormonal flirting conversations? If so, be happy. If you hear meanness or bullying type conversations remember to talk to your child once they are alone with you. NEVER talk to your child in front of their friends if at all possible. Your child has a need to save face in front of their peers. Do not put them in an awkward spot. Talk to them later in general ways, never leading on that you heard their conversation. Try to appeal to their feelings. They have a lot of those at this age! Share with them how you feel about a related topic. Then release your child and his/her friends to the hands of God where they come from. Have faith that their minds will be healed even if their behavior doesn't appear to be.

4)   Technology

Technology is intertwined with their social life and their friendships. Trying to control it is asking for suffering by both parent and child. It is the medium by which children today keep in contact with one another. There are however, things that can be done to keep it safe.

Make sure you have talked frankly about the dangers of the internet. Let your child know that foolish decisions made using the internet can never be taken back or fixed. Stress that your child take a few minutes to think about what they are saying or posting online before they do it. This is a time to start to verbalize your morals to your child. They will appear to not listen to what you are saying but statistically kids this age do not stray too far from what their family values are.

This is a time of experimentation in many areas so errors will be made. Like the toddler, they have to manipulate their world to learn from it. They may find themselves in situations they do not know how to get out of. If your child feels that you are open and nonjudgmental they are more apt to come to you when they have questions or are in trouble. Try very, very hard not to react if this happens. Turn within for a second before you respond to your child. Respectfully an calmly answer the question or comment. If they need help, offer what you can. If there is a consequence because of a mistake they made, let them experience it. It is hard to watch your child suffer a consequence as a result of their behavior but it part of the growing experience. Release it to the Holy Spirit knowing that it is already healed even if the form of this world still appears to be in chaos. This too shall pass!

5)   Attitude

Middle age school children's attitudes can be looked at one of two ways. It can be frustrating and annoying or it can be humorous and viewed as a moment in time that will be gone in a second. As parents and part of the Sonship we get to decide how we want to perceive things. You will get lots of practice with attitudes of young teenagers.

This is the age of rolling eyes, heavy sighs, and outright ignoring. Tones become sarcastic and argumentative. From a **Course** perspective we all live behind the veil. The true essence of your child is not the attitudinal individual in front of you. The Christ of your Child is not anything you see. Hold that thought during the teenage temper tantrums.

During this time try to view your child as an actor portraying a role as a temperamental middle school age child. Your child's character is scripted to stomp their feet, whine and roll their eyes. Bravo! What a terrific performance! Know that when the show is over, the actor is nothing like the character they portray in the show. That's the Truth of who your child is. He/she is a precious Child of God in Whom He is well pleased. He/she is perfectly holy. God does not attend theatrical events and does not know of such a character. Things are Divinely perfect. Relax!

6)   Peer Pressure

Peer Pressure is at its worst during the middle or junior high years. Children this age are muddling through life trying to find their roles in life and they are relying on others who are also muddling through. It is literally the blind leading the blind. Again, you have to allow most of it to evolve like it will. When you interfere you are saying your plan for salvation will work. The **Course** says only God's plan for salvation will work. We spend a lot of time trying to figure things out when in Truth we do not need to. When we take control we are telling God that we know better than Him. That is arrogance!

Your job as parents is to communicate as nonjudgmentally as possible your thoughts and desires about behaviors typical to young teens and then stand back and catch them if they fall. When you see them choosing wisely according to your perception, it is good to tell them you notice their maturity. Encourage your child to think for him/herself instead of going along with those who they may not agree with.

This is a crucial time for parental modeling. Your child will get many more messages from your behavior instead of your comments. If you are not thinking for yourself and going along with friends or co-workers then you cannot expect your child to do so. If you are gossiping about someone in a judgmental way you cannot expect your child not to do so. You have to live the values you believe. It is time to do some cleaning up of your own behaviors and attitudes.

7) More Sneaky Behavior

Sneaky behavior starts much younger than at this stage of development but it reaches its peak during the teen years. Nothing upsets parents more than to find out their child has done something with the pure intention to hide it from them. The reason why your child does sneaky things is what should give parents food for thought.

Adults do sneaky things too so parents need to think about why they may do something without the knowledge of the people closest to them. Sometimes it's because the action is either immoral. The hope in this case is that by keeping quiet the behavior won't be caught by others. At other times, it's because they do not want to cause emotion in another. Regardless of the reason, the person committing the deed has personal motives for keeping their behaviors to themselves.

In the case of teenagers, it usually is because they do not want the judgment of their parents. The fact that they are being sneaky tells you that they know their actions are not good. Children are open and honest about actions that are appropriate. So the questions becomes, what do you do about behaviors that you do not want your child to do?

There is no clear-cut answer to this. The **Course** would tell you that it is not your job in their world to change a brother. As a parent you probably do not want to hear this. However, it may be just the thing you need to do. Send loving healing thoughts to your child. Mentally release your child into the loving hands of God, knowing they are perfectly whole regardless of the insane behavior they are displaying.

In the world, make sure to model the behavior you would like your child to display. Express your values as nonjudgmentally as possible. Help your child get out of any messes they get themselves into without lecturing and condemning. Let them experience the consequences of any action they choose. In your mind, bring them to the Light of Love.

Middle or junior high school aged children are challenging to say the least. Know that this is a few years that could be filled with suffering or could be filled with joy. It all depends on how you see things. The choice is yours.

Chapter Seven

Age 15 Through Age 18

The high school years can be a fun and exciting time for your child or it can be a period of suffering and pain. Unfortunately, as his/her parent you have no control over how your child will view and experience their world.

1)   Reasonableness

Much of the unreasonableness of middle or junior high school is beginning to fade away and the child you wanted to send away to an island or sell to gypsies is returning to normalcy. This age can be delightful for parents as they watch their soon-to-be adult children experience things they were not able to before now.

It can also be a time of heartache as parents watch their child suffer with school and friendships. One can honestly say there is nothing in this world that simulates high school. Many children struggle to find an environment where they fit in. This can lead to misuse of drugs, alcohol, or other inappropriate behaviors. Because of their mental abilities at this age, it becomes difficult for parents to intervene when they see their child going down a dangerous path.

The good news is most high school teens are beginning to make their own choices about their lives. As a parent, you are seeing the values your child has developed when you watch their actions.

Their personalities and the things they have seen modeled by their family will determine how they are viewing their world. If as a parent you see things that you believe are your fault, remember to allow errors in yourself as well as in your teen.

Parents often turn their focus to feeling guilty for any inadequacies they perceive they have had while raising their children. As mentioned before, the **Course** tells you that you are the perfect Child of God in whom He is well pleased. That principle applies to parents too!

2)   More Independence

What parents with children this age must remember is that you do not get to choose the path your child decides he/she is going to take. Even if you do not want to give your child more independence because of the bad choices they are making, you will not be able to stop the inevitability of their independent lives, separate from you.

The most you can do is to let your child know your wishes for them and then allow them to go forward. Parents are often surprised at how their children actually make reasonable decisions about their lives when parents love and trust in their ability to do so. I believe the key to success with most high school children is to practice loving them despite their outwardly behaviors.

Parents that are themselves living through the eyes of fear instead of Love, see all the dangers of the world causing them to worry about their teens. This is counterproductive. It does not stop your child from doing things they believe they must do. Trying to protect your adolescent through controlling seldom accomplishes the results you would hope for.

This is time when parents have to trust or have faith in their children as individuals. Mistakes will be made but if we are truthful with ourselves, it's mistakes that helped us to learn. This is the same for our children. They have to make their own mistakes. Parents, as practicing teachers of the

Course know that there are no REAL mistakes so we are comfortable letting go of the reigns of our youth.

The ***Course*** teaches that there is a Christ in all of us that is really who we are. The body, ego-mind, and worldly behaviors that we see our brothers do (including your child), are not the Truth of who they are. Remembering to see past the veil of the body is crucial for helping parents cope with the high school years.

3) Encouragement Without Interfering

Teenagers are very sensitive to parental judgment. Giving advice or encouragement can be very tricky and parents need to pay close attention to how and what they say to their kids. When teens open up about ideas or plans they have, parents need to turn within and ask for guidance from the Holy Spirit before opening their mouths! The old saying, "you get more bees with honey" is apropos here. Try to find ways of getting whatever message of encouragement or advice out in a way that is not lecturing or judging. Showing confidence in your child to do what is right for him/her is important. Your child will not feel controlled and is more likely to make a sound, reasonable decision.

During the next ten years of your child's life, they will make many decisions only to change or modify their decisions based on experience or knowledge gained. This is a good thing. This means your child is aware of his/her errors and is making better decisions. There are many adults who are incapable of doing this so if your teen is showing signs of this, be grateful!

4)   Sexuality

One of the decisions your child will be faced with during this phase in their lives is when to have their first sexual experience. This frightens many parents needlessly. The reality of this world is that the overwhelming majority of people will eventually have sex. Sex is part of life in form. I think what frightens parents the most is the possibility of pregnancy or the possibility of sexually transmitted diseases. My guidance tells me that if children at this age do not have accurate information about the prevention of pregnancy and sexually transmitted diseases they cannot make reasonable decisions regarding sex. We all know parents who were "abstinent only" types and tried to push that morality onto their children. Anything that is pushed on kids at this age group usually causes rebellious behavior. I believe it is more important to give your child "real" information about sex along with your thoughts about it in a non-judgmental way.

However, let your child know that if they make the decision to have their first sexual encounter that you will assist them so they can avoid any unwanted results from the experience. This trust you are relaying to your child often produces a delay in their first sexual activity. But let's be real; most people have had sex by the age of eighteen. Look at your own generation. Most parents have had their first sexual encounter by the age of eighteen or nineteen. Expecting anything different of our children is hypocritical. They have the same sexual energies so expecting them to wait until they are married never was realistic.

5) More Sneaky Behavior

I see the sneaky behavior of this stage of development a little bit different than that of previous stages. While some of the unknown activities of your teens are because they know you would not approve, many are because they are developing their individual lives. Parents often take this personally as offensive but it's part of the evolvement of humans in the world the ego developed.

It's difficult for parents to understand that they no longer need to know everything going on in their teen's life. They do not need to know every thought or emotion in their child's seemingly separate mind. Understanding this helps transition both parent and child to adulthood where parents have to sever the cord of attachment. This is much more emotional for parents than it is for their children. Leaning on the *Course* for comfort and knowledge will assist with this shift.

The *Course* would encourage you to see your teenager as another brother who is one with you. This is an important time to back away from the attachment you feel as a parent and begin viewing them as part of the One Mind. Know that the Holy Spirit heals their errors the instant they occur. In Truth, there is no time and the events of this world are instantly healed when we release them to the Christ within us.

Chapter Eight

Age 19 Through Age 25

Your child will be developing a plan for their lives during this stage of development. It may differ from the plan you had for their lives. According to the **Course**, neither plan will work because only God's plan for your life will work. That does not mean that no action occurs in the human realm because it does. It simply means that whatever action you or your adult child does, it will be corrected by Holy Spirit even if it does not appear to be fixed in our perception.

1) Ego-centric AGAIN

There are three times in a child's development when their ego-focused tendencies are more prominent. The first is during the toddler years. The second is during the middle school years. And the last, in my opinion, is during the early adult years. During this time in their lives, they appear to only be able to think of what they want. Their actions often seem to be insensitive to the needs of others.

Young adults have the legal right to make their own decisions but they often don't have the developmental ability to foresee the consequences of those decisions. The scare for parents is that judicially they can have more serious consequences than ever before. There is nothing I can say to change or alleviate those concerns for parents. This is a time when having faith in the principles of the **Course** will help. You have to decide to either believe the **Course** or not. Knowing that your child is really not a separate person making whatever choices they are can provide comfort and peace.

Your legal adult child has rights they did not have before and they are detaching themselves from you at a rapid pace. Parental egos want to be offended by this. Our egos tell us they do not love or respect us. Nothing is further from the truth. If you remember back to when you were that age. You may not have shown that you loved and respected your parents but in retrospect, you know you did. The same is true for the young adult that is your child. Whatever feelings they believe they have for their parents at the time, know that those will change as they age. As long as you remember the Truth of who they are, you as parents can find the peace your ego will attempt to steal from you.

    2)   Letting Go

Total release will never occur from your child while you are in a body in the world. But learning to let go of responsibility for the things your grown child is doing must happen. If you continue to view your now adult child like you did when they were underage, you will experience nothing but suffering and pain.

It is hard to watch your child grown up and experience the ups and downs of life. It's hard to watch them make decisions that you know may cause them agony. Yet watch you must. You can still try to offer advice based on your own perspective and experience but your child has no obligation to follow or listen to that advice. You will always have the right to express nonjudgmental opinions or stories of experience but beyond that, you must allow your adult child to make their own decisions. Holding grievances related to those choices only keeps you in a state of pain. True forgiveness will heal any misperceptions and set all you look upon free.

3) Pooper Scooper

This is what I felt like I was doing during this time in my own children's lives. I was powerless to affect their decisions and felt like all I could do was walk behind them with the pooper-scooper, trying to help them clean up the mess after the fact.

Of course, this is not true. I now know I did not need to do that. It was a conscious choice on my part. There are times when you will joyfully want to carry the pooper-scooper and assist your child in fixing whatever mess presents itself, like you would a good friend. There are other times however, you might be carrying the shovel, picking up the soiled mess and feeling nothing but resentment because your ego believes you would not have to do this if your child had listened to your advice. The **Course** reminds you that you can always choose again. If you do not like the decision or action you are taking, choose again. You can put down the pooper-scooper at any time. Putting it down is a metaphor for letting resentment and grievances go.

4) Tying up Loose Ends

This is the proper time to choose new rules for the relationship with your now adult child. The co-dependencies of the past must be abolished and a new connection for the future must be established. At first your child might seem shocked when the safety net is not there when he/she expected it to be. That's okay. This will be a time of many new first time experiences. Both sides of the coin will need to adapt to the different expectations, hopefully without judgment.

Your child may find it hurtful when you detach. You have to realize that that is his/her perception of you and you can and should do nothing. According to the **Course** you are not here to change the world but to change your perception of the world as you slowly come out of the dream. Accepting that your adult child is also coming out of the dream but at his/her own pace can be frustrating. In **Course** terms your relationship with your child (or anyone for that matter) is to change the special relationship into a holy relationship. You have to offer forgiveness to others for what they have done. Rest in God knowing that everything is taken care for according to His Will.

5) Mental Illness

During the late teen and early twenties we often begin to see signs of mental illness if it is part of the human body's physiology. Most parents will not experience the effects of a child with mental illness. This section is only for those who do.

Mental illness, according to the **Course** does not exist outside of all perceived illness. While I personally believe that, when you experience it, it does seem very different. The *Course* says that all illness is mental illness. In our western culture, that does not seem so. Cancer and bipolar disorder seem like two very different kinds of illness. Yet I challenge you to look again at this.

Mental illness is something I have become very familiar with. The ego mind judges mental illness very differently than it does physical illness. Up until recently, mental illness had little or no coverage in most health insurance policies. That coverage varies greatly from state to state and policy to policy. Because of the differences, public opinion varies as well. Knowing the Truth the *Course* curriculum teaches, we know that all these differences are nothing more that ego judgments.

If you have to act because your child is mentally ill, your peace and faith can be shook to the core. Their behavior can be erratic and bizarre. Law enforcement and mental health authorities may have to be called upon. Initially you may have to take more control of your mentally ill child than would normally be the case for a person this age. Your *Course* study may grind to a halt as you delve deeply into your ego's fear.

My hope is that you eventually awaken to the realization that like with an adult child who is not mentally ill, you cannot control the path they choose to take either. The law will allow them to make their own decisions. That includes whether to seek treatment or not. Since the **Course** does not discourage treatment of any kind, it does imply that it is nothing more than magic. I am not saying that mentally ill individuals should not seek treatment if they are called to. My opinion is that a mentally ill person by worldly standards may actually be more awake in this world than we give them credit for if they refuse treatment. This is a perspective not shared by many.

If you experience mental illness with your child or any family member, like mentioned many times before in this book, try to remember the Truth of who they are. Love the Christ in them without believing the insane actions their ego bodies are doing. That does not mean you do not take action when action is needed. If the police must be called for you or your child's protection, do that. But do it with Holy Spirit's vision. Get quiet if only for a minute and ask for guidance. Surrender back to one of the beginning lessons in the **Course** workbook that teaches you do not know what anything means. Only God's plan for your mentally ill child's salvation will work. Trust that your child is being Divinely cared for.

Chapter Nine

Adult Children

At this point in your adult child's life, they are functioning in the world of form on their own. They may be married and have children. They have jobs, a mortgage and responsibilities. They have their own beliefs and opinions. Your relationship with your adult child will depend on the things you have done thus far.

1) Helping, But Not Too Much

Finally your adult children are living their own lives. Even if they are still living with you in your house, they are doing their own thing for the most part. Your ability to affect the trajectory of their lives is less and less apparent. They are not as self-centered as they were in their early adult years. This can be a nice time if you allow them to be exactly who they are.

Now that your children are running their own lives, they may yearn for the days when you helped out a little more. Some adult children might try to manipulate you into taking on some of their responsibilities and problem solving. This can become troublesome if you allow it to.

When your adult child asks you for help, do not automatically say yes. Do not allow your child to manipulate you into doing something you do not want to do out of guilt. Do not give in because of their whining. The best thing you can do is to stop parenting altogether.

I have heard many parents say, "You never stop parenting!" I think I may have said that myself. That's a belief and because it's only a belief, it can be changed. The truth is you still have the option to help your child. If you are asked to assist, take time before answering. Surrender to the Christ within you, knowing you will be guided into Right action. If that guidance is to help, do so with gladness in your heart. If you are guided to decline, know that regardless of the disappointment your child may display, it too is the Right action. Detach from the emotion remembering that it is not the Truth of who you are.

2) Staying in Your Own Yard

One of my favorite lecturers and authors Jacob Glass talks frequently about staying in your own yard. This is a simple way of saying mind your own business! This is alignment with the *Course* that teaches your only purpose is to heal your own mind. The *Course* also talks about the way back to God is with your brother. If you are in someone else's yard, minding someone else's business, you believe you are separate from your brother. In Truth you are One with your brother so by staying in your own yard and healing your own perspective you are also healing the mind of your brother. To love your brother all you have to do is Love yourself!

When it comes to your adult children, staying in your own yard is much more difficult. That's because we still believe our grown children are special. The *Course* says they are no more special than the stranger standing in front of you at the grocery store. When you finally feel that the message of the *Course* is true, you begin to view those unknown to you with the same Love you use to view your kids. The nice thing is, when you are seeing your family as special, all you have to do is choose again.

In this world, there are going to be people you spend more time with than others. That does not make them special. In God's eyes they are all the same because they are all part of the Sonship, the One Mind. Enjoy the moments you have with them without special attachment. Love them as you would love anyone else. The more you can grow to do this, the more peace and happiness you will experience.

3) Giving Up Judgments

Once our children are grown and have families of their own, it is our job to catch ourselves when we are judging them. They may not be doing the career we think they should. They may not be raising their children the way we think is appropriate. We may not be happy with the morals they are practicing. But here is the question . . . who gets to decide who is right and who is wrong? Yes, there are worldly laws we have to live by but even those can be open to interpretation. That's why we have courts. That's why we have juries. But in the world of parenting, there's a lot of wiggle room.

We basically have two choices as aging parents. We can stand in judgment of our children and others or we can be happy and have peace. We cannot have both. So which one do you choose?

4) Grandchildren

I thought I was doing really well with the special relationship ideas in the *Course* and then grandchildren came along.

When you are a parent with small children you do not think there is anyone you can love more than your own children. Grandchildren challenge that belief. So applying the thought of no special relationships to my grandchildren took a lot of effort.

I believe that grandchildren are the ego's last, ditch attempt to hold on to power. If you can somehow surrender the idea that your grandchildren are no more special than any other child, it wins. But like the ***Course*** says, this is a lifelong study. If you don't learn to love your grandchildren like you love every brother, you will lose the peace of God along with your happiness.

If however, you can begin to unlearn this special relationship concept, more and more joy and happiness can be in your life. As I began to look at my grandbabies as the Children of God, I began to feel love for them that I had not experienced before. I still have parental tendencies to worry, protect, and control them. Loving myself, as soon as I realize I am doing that, I release them to the loving hands of God and ask for my peace back. I need do nothing but enjoy these seemingly individual little beings with total Love and my moments in their company are pure Heaven.

The urge to judge their parents and how they are parenting will rear its ugly head many times but he always have the opportunity to surrender those thoughts and choose peace again. Do not judge yourself for having those thoughts. If you love others but not yourself, you can love no one!

5) Mental Illness And Addictions

Let me briefly touch once again on the topic of mental illness and addictions. If your grown child has a humanly diagnosis of mental illness and addiction, you could spend a lot of time fighting with yourself about how to see this situation. I can only give you my thoughts I have received from my Higher Power about this.

When a situation occurs that is fear based and not Love based, I try to remember that what my human eyes see is not what God knows to be Truth. The individual who appears to be mentally ill or suffering from addiction is only the outwardly expression of the separation from God. The minute I remember that that individual is ME and I am HIM/HER I forgive my perception of the actions that that person seems to be doing.
My path to God is with my brother.

Chapter Ten

And So It Is

A Course in Miracles is a self study course designed to make your believe in the separation from God less painful while you are experiencing it. Gradually you awaken from the dream that you are separate from God and your brothers. Gradually you learn to recognize the difference between Love based thoughts and fear based thoughts. Heaven is within and we each have constant opportunities to choose the thoughts we want.

Using ***A Course in Miracles*** as a foundation when parenting can help you navigate the issues that will arise without as much pain and suffering. It will not mean that you will be problem free. On the contrary, problems will still occur as always. What will be different is how you see them and how you feel when they are happening. That is the value of the ***Course***.

As long as we believe we are our bodies, you will never be totally in your Right Mind. I think when the time comes you will lay the body down because there will be no need for it. In the meantime, my hope is to experience more and more moments of total peace and joy. The more I study the **Course**, the shorter the space between those moments.

While writing this I turned within for Divine guidance about what to suggest in any given situation. I am not suggesting that you need to do anything I have talked about. Take what feels right to you and leave the rest. There are lots of parenting books out there. Only you know what feels like Love to you.

When it comes to parenting, I believe we do the best we can, based on what we know at the time. The **Course** says that all errors are already healed. Rest in the peace of God and know who walks with you wherever you go. Amen.

Made in the USA
San Bernardino, CA
10 October 2015